Bess Press Inc.
3565 Harding Avenue
Honolulu, HI 96816

Creative and Production by Pass-the-Projects Inc.
Design by Joseph Abad Jr.

Publisher's Cataloging-in-Publication Data

Names: Cataluna, Lee.
Title: Ordinary ohana / Lee Cataluna.
Description: Honolulu : Bess Press, 2016. | Summary: This is a little book about a big family that
        makes the point that family is who you chose and there's always room for more at Sunday dinner,
        even if it's on Saturday night.
Identifiers: ISBN 978-1-57306-527-6 (hardcover)
Subjects: LCSH: Picture books for children. | CYAC: Hawaii--Fiction. | Families--Fiction. | Family
        life--Fiction. | Multiculturalism--Fiction. | BISAC: JUVENILE FICTION / Boys & Men. |
        JUVENILE FICTION / Family / General.
Classification: LCC PZ7.C252125 Or 2016 (print) | LCC PZ7.C252125 (ebook) | DDC [Fic]--dc23.

isbn: 978-1-57306-513-9

Printed in China
BessPress.com

ORDINARY 'OHANA

written by Lee Cataluna
illustrated by Cheyne Gallarde

published by Bess Press

I don't have an ordinary family.

I live in Hawai‘i.

I have an

'OHANA

We live with my Grandma Alice in a big house.

We used to live on the bottom floor, but then Grandma Alice said she was tired of going upstairs, so we switched.

木刻箸

CHOP STICK

Everybody comes over for Sunday dinner. Sometimes, we have Sunday dinner on Saturday night.

Or Wednesday.

Or whenever.

Everybody brings something.

I have an
Aunty Darling
and a
Cousin Darling.

Hello
my name is
Aunty D

My grandma calls them
Big Darling and Small Darling.

I call them Aunty D and "Hey, you!"

(Just kidding. I call my cousin Darling "Cousin Darling.")

We have five Kainoas — my grandpa, my uncle, two cousins and me.

When somebody calls, **"Kainoa!"**

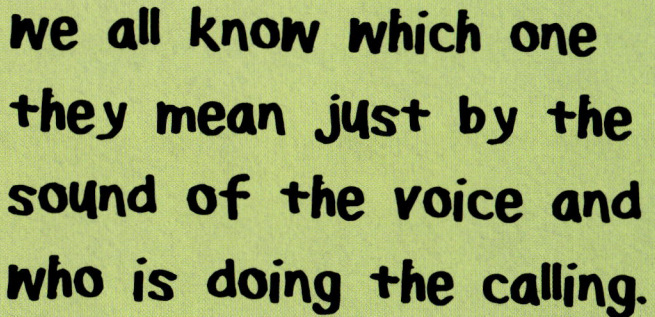

We all know which one they mean just by the sound of the voice and who is doing the calling.

I have an Aunty Angie
who isn't an aunty-aunty.
She's my mom's partner
and my second mom.

This is my dad's hanai sister who is really his cousin. He calls her Cousin Tita. We call her Aunty Cousin Tita. She always brings coconut cake.

Terri-Lynn is my second cousin. Or third cousin. I just call her cousin.

LOL!

knock-knock!

She doesn't walk or talk but she likes to laugh, so I sit by her wheelchair and tell her my best jokes.

I have a half-brother from my dad's wife named Daniel.

I have a step-brother from Aunty Angie named David.

David and Daniel get to be brothers because of me.

This is my Uncle Boo.
He can barbecue anything,
even a Thanksgiving turkey.

These are my California cousins. We send them care packages of stuff from here.

They send us care packages of stuff from there.

ess Box

My baby cousin Rosie came from China.

My mom's cousin's wife Rosemary is from Wisconsin.

My Aunty Rosie came from the Philippines.

WISCONSIN

They all came from far away but now they are related.

If I ever get confused,
this is how I remember:

My 'ohana is all the people who came to the hospital when Grandpa was sick.

My 'ohana is all the people who brought lei when my cousin Kainoa graduated from college.

My 'ohana is everyone who bought laulau when I had a school fundraiser.

GO GO GO!

My 'ohana is everyone who is paddling the canoe and everyone cheering for us from shore.

My ʻohana is all the names I bless in my prayers. Sometimes it takes a long time to say my prayers.

I know.
Pretty ordinary.

This is
my 'ohana

'ohana photos here